1 9 8 4
The Year I Was Born

Compiled by Sally Tagholm

Illustrated by Michael Evans

FANTAIL

in association with Signpost Books

FANTAIL PUBLISHING, AN IMPRINT OF PUFFIN ENTERPRISES
Published by the Penguin Group
27 Wrights Lane London W8 5TZ, England
Viking Penguin Inc., 40 West 23rd Street, New York, NY 10010, USA
Penguin Books Australia, Ltd., Ringwood, Victoria, Australia
Penguin Books Canada, Ltd., 2801 John Street, Markham, Ontario,
Canada L3R 1B4
Penguin Books Ltd., Registered Offices: Harmondsworth, Middlesex,
England
Published by Fantail Books in association with Signpost Books

First published 1990
10 9 8 7 6 5 4 3 2 1

Based on an original idea by Sally Wood
Conceived, designed and produced by Signpost Books, Ltd 1989
Copyright in this format © 1990 Signpost Books Ltd.,
44 Uxbridge Street London W8 7TG
England

Illustrations copyright © 1990 Michael Evans
Text copyright © 1990 Sally Tagholm

Pasteup: Naomi Games
Editor: Dorothy Wood

ISBN 0140 90202 3

Colour separations by Fotographics, Ltd.
Printed and bound in Belgium by Proost Book Production through
Landmark Production Consultants, Ltd.

Typeset by AKM Associates (UK) Ltd, Ajmal House, Hayes Road,
Southall, London

ME

Name:
Date of birth:
Time of birth:
Place of birth:
Weight at birth:
Colour of eyes:
Colour of hair (if any):
Distinguishing marks:

Mum

Dad

Sister/Brother

Sister/Brother

MY FAMILY

January

Sunday January 1

Eric Peters from Littlehampton, Sussex, sets off from Putney to sail round the world in a barrel, but turns back after a few minutes with engine trouble.

Monday January 2

Bank Holiday. A record number of 80 turkeys, ducks and geese have been saved from the Christmas oven at Wingshaven, a bird sanctuary in Sussex.

Tuesday January 3

The Prince of Wales falls off his horse while out with the Cottesmore Hunt in Leicestershire. Buckingham Palace announces that women will not be allowed into the Royal enclosure at Ascot if their hats are too small.

New Moon

Wednesday January 4

A new pirate radio station called *Laser 7.30am* goes on the air from the Thames Estuary.

Thursday January 5

A nationwide treasure hunt for 12 golden eggs is launched by Cadbury's. William Derby (13) of Alford, Surrey, is presented with the first 22-carat egg worth £10,000!

Friday January 6

Edinburgh Zoo launches an Adoption Scheme for animals: a crocodile costs £90 per year.

Saturday January 7

A special calendar for 1984 has been made from inner London school-children's paintings of their teachers: this month features Mrs Brenda Malyan, head of Honeywell School in Wandsworth.

Sunday January 8

The Mad Hatter's Christmas Party at the Grosvenor House Hotel in London. Happy 100th Birthday to Mrs Rose Healey in Middleton, Northamptonshire.

Monday January 9

A black miniature poodle called Champion Filigran, the Master of Valetta, wins the Pup of the Year 1984 title.

Tuesday January 10

Richard Broadhead, who turned back to rescue a French competitor in last year's single-handed round-the-world yacht race, is presented with the Yachtsman of the Year Award.

Wednesday January 11

A small wooden toy army hut is sold for £700 at Phillips auction rooms in London.

Thursday January 12

A stormy night with heavy rain! It's the wettest January in England and Wales since 1948.

Friday January 13

Hurricane force winds! A 114m-high cooling tower collapses near Warrington in Cheshire. RAF men rescue French trawlermen off the Irish coast.

January

Named after the Roman god, Janus, who had two faces and could look backwards and forwards at the same time. Also known as 'frosty month', 'wolf month', 'after yule', 'first month' and 'snow month'.

A fossilized fish, more than 2m long, was found at the end of last year in a claypit near Peterborough. This month, the Natural History Museum in London identify it as belonging to the genus ASTHENOCORMOUS! It is at least 150,000,000 years old!

A Birthday Brush-up in New York

The Statue of Liberty, in New York Harbour, will celebrate her 100th birthday in 1986. To make sure she looks her best, huge scaffolding is sprouting all the way round her so that she can be cleaned and repaired in time. She is over 46m tall and stands on a pedestal that makes her 93m high. There is an observation platform right at the top of her head!

Saturday *January 14*	Jayne Torvill and Christopher Dean win their third European ice-dance title in 4 years in Budapest.
Sunday *January 15*	Helicopters drop food and supplies to people stranded by torrential rain and flooding in central and northern Australia.
Monday *January 16*	A chimpanzee called Poppy is born to Meg and Boris at Chester Zoo.
Tuesday *January 17*	The Needles Lighthouse keepers, stranded by heavy seas since Friday, are rescued by a Royal Navy helicopter. They have been on duty for 33 days!
Wednesday *January 18*	Arthur Ransome, who wrote *Swallows and Amazons*, was born in Leeds 100 years ago today. Full Moon
Thursday *January 19*	The Christmas mail arrives at Inishbofin (population 11), a tiny island off the coast of Donegal: it was delayed by stormy seas! The 900th anniversary of Worcester Cathedral.
Friday *January 20*	The International Contemporary Art Fair opens in London: one of the sculptures is made with 1800 HP Sauce bottles! –20.6°C at Aviemore, Scotland
Saturday *January 21*	Johnny Weissmuller, who played Tarzan, dies aged 79. Travellers are trapped in cars and trains by snow in Scotland and the north of England.
Sunday *January 22*	Sponsored endurance test in the icy Serpentine in Hyde Park, London, by members of the Holborn Sub-Aqua Club!
Monday *January 23*	No school today for pupils at Kingussie High School in Scotland—they're snowed up!
Tuesday *January 24*	Seventeen seamen drown after abandoning ship in gales off Guernsey.
Wednesday *January 25*	Mrs Thatcher inspects a cardboard igloo and other equipment for *Operation Raleigh*, a round-the-world youth expedition which starts later this year.
Thursday *January 26*	Australia Day. Lord Shinwell becomes Pipeman of the Century and Henry Cooper Pipeman of the Year. Whirlwind in Teignmouth, Devon. Arctic weather in Scotland and the north
Friday *January 27*	Rivers burst their banks in Devon and Somerset: the London to West Country railway line is closed.

Saturday *January 28*	Sponsored relay run by policemen and women from Hull to London to raise money for people who were hurt when a bomb exploded outside Harrods last December.
Sunday *January 29*	The Olympic torch is lit from the sun's rays at Olympia in Greece and starts its journey to Sarajevo in Yugoslavia for the Winter Games. 
Monday *January 30*	A lifeboat is stationed at Alderney in the Channel Isles for the first time in 100 years.
Tuesday *January 31*	The one-legged Lincoln Imp, who has been the official emblem of Lincoln County Council for 10 years, is given the sack.

January 17th
The Post Office issues 4 new stamps to celebrate the 500th anniversary of the College of Arms

January 31st
THE LINCOLN IMP
According to local legend, the Lincoln Imp was sent by the Devil to cause trouble on earth. He was turned to stone in the 11th century and, to this day, stares down from the ceiling of Lincoln Cathedral, surrounded by angels!

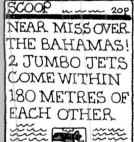 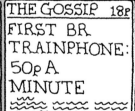  

SCOOP ~~~~~ 20p
NEAR MISS OVER THE BAHAMAS! 2 JUMBO JETS COME WITHIN 180 METRES OF EACH OTHER.

THE GOSSIP 18p
FIRST BR TRAINPHONE: 50p A MINUTE

CHIT-CHAT 22p
EMPEROR PENGUIN NESTS DESTROYED IN ANTARCTICA BY NEW AIR STRIP

DAILY SCANDAL 19p
SUPERTED BOUGHT BY DISNEY CABLE CHANNEL!

February

Wednesday February 1	The Chancellor of the Exchequer announces that the ½p coin will disappear by the end of the year. New Moon
Thursday February 2	Beginning of the Chinese Year of the Rat. Two West Indian turtles have been washed up in Perranporth and Hayle in Cornwall.
Friday February 3	The US space shuttle Challenger is launched, with a 5-man crew on board, from Cape Canaveral, Florida.
Saturday February 4	An official Duck Minder has been appointed at Ramsay, Cambridgeshire: salary £250 per year!
Sunday February 5	Annual Clown Service at Holy Trinity Church, Dalston, East London, in memory of the great clown Grimaldi.
Monday February 6	Blood taken from Chia-Chia, the Giant Panda at London Zoo, is flown to the seriously ill Tjen-Tjen in West Berlin zoo.
Tuesday February 7	The first unattached space walk! US astronaut Bruce McCandless floats at 8km a second away from the space shuttle Challenger, 265km above earth!
Wednesday February 8	The 14th Winter Olympics open at Sarajevo, Yugoslavia. Three Soviet cosmonauts are launched in a Soyuz space capsule. With the 5 US astronauts on board Challenger, there are now 8 men in space—a new record! Worst gales for 10 years
Thursday February 9	Yuri Andropov, leader of the Soviet Communist party, dies. A herd of deer has caused 3 accidents in the last week on roads between Holt and Sheringham in Norfolk!
Friday February 10	Crufts Dog Show opens in London: 10,272 entries this year! Harold Macmillan, who was Prime Minister between 1957 and 1963, is 90 today: he is given an earldom!
Saturday February 11	US space shuttle Challenger lands on a 4.8km runway at the Kennedy Space Centre in Florida for the first time.
Sunday February 12	Hank, a 4-year-old Lhasa Apso, a Tibetan Royal dog, wins the Supreme Champion title at Crufts in London.
Monday February 13	Happy 30th Birthday to the Bash Street Gang in the comic *Beano*! The Prince and Princess of Wales announce that they are expecting their second baby in September.
Tuesday February 14	St Valentine's Day. Elton John (real name Reg Dwight) marries Renate Blauel in Sydney, Australia.

February

The Roman month of purification. The name comes from the Latin 'februo' which means 'I purify by sacrifice'. It has also been known as 'sprout kale' and 'rain month'.

January
February
March
April
May
June
July
August
September

October
November
December
Monday
Tuesday
Wednesday
Thursday
Friday
Saturday
Sunday

LEAP YEAR

Ordinary Year	Leap Year
12 months	12 months
52 weeks	52 weeks
365 days	366 days

Leap years are one day longer than ordinary years because it takes the earth slightly more than 365 days to go round the sun—365.242 days, to be precise! An extra day (February 29) is added every four years to even things up on the calendar. This means that anyone born on February 29 only has one birthday every four years!

Chinese Year of the Rat

According to legend, the Buddha summoned all the animals in the world to him one New Year, and promised them all a reward. Only twelve obeyed and he gave them each a year: the Rat arrived first so he got the first year! The order of the 12-year cycle is always the same: Rat, Buffalo, Tiger, Cat, Dragon, Snake, Horse, Goat, Monkey, Cockerel, Dog and Pig.
  Rats are very charming, imaginative and creative. They are also very honest. They can be nervous, restless and aggressive, however, and sometimes have quick tempers! Good partners for Rats are Dragons and Buffaloes but NOT Cats or Horses! Famous Rats include William Shakespeare, Jules Verne, Mozart and Winston Churchill.

THE WINTER OLYMPICS
1,590 competitors from 49 different countries take part in the Winter Olympics at Sarajevo in Yugoslavia. Torvill and Dean win a gold medal for Britain for ice dancing on St Valentine's Day.

Wednesday *February 15*	Emergency repairs are carried out to the pier at Weston-super-Mare after a pontoon crashes into it.
Thursday *February 16*	Eric the Orang Utan is being renamed Erica, after unexpectedly giving birth at Chicago Zoo!
Friday *February 17*	Roads in France are blocked by lorry drivers protesting against a go-slow strike by customs officers at both ends of the Mont Blanc tunnel. The Lincoln Imp is reprieved! (see Jan 31) Full Moon
Saturday *February 18*	There are now 5,173 man-made objects floating in space! 1,329 are orbiting satellites, 50 are deep-space probes and the rest is 'junk'.
Sunday *February 19*	US twins Phil and Steve Mahre make Olympic history in Sarajevo by finishing first and second in the men's slalom.
Monday *February 20*	An electronic nose, called a High-Tech Hooter, is being developed at Warwick University, to sniff out bad food and dangerous gases.
Tuesday *February 21*	An M4 sliproad near Newbury, Berkshire, is blocked for more than 5 hours by 10 tonnes of mussels from an overturned lorry.
Wednesday *February 22*	Police are searching for an iguana on the Isle of Wight, after finding a tail more than 90 cms long at Newport!
Thursday *February 23*	World's biggest traffic jam in France because of blockading lorries. (see Feb 17) Formal independence celebrations in Brunei.
Friday *February 24*	French lorry drivers lift the blockades and traffic starts to move!
Saturday *February 25*	The Royal Mint has struck a special gold HK$1,000 dollar coin (about £90) to commemorate the Chinese Year of the Rat. Hammersmith Bridge in London cracks!
Sunday *February 26*	Rare sighting of an Asian olive-backed pipit from Siberia in Bracknell, Berkshire.
Monday *February 27*	An electric bike with a top speed of 24kph is launched in Birmingham.
Tuesday *February 28*	The Prince of Wales names a new research ship, the *RRS Charles Darwin*, at Appledore Ship Yard in Devon.
Wednesday *February 29*	Leap Year Day. Happy 100th Birthday to Joe Cresswell, of Thurmaston, near Leicester! This is only the 24th time he has been able to celebrate.

March

Thursday *March 1*	The Government bans trade unions at the top-secret intelligence HQ at Cheltenham. St David's Day!
Friday *March 2*	A live colorado beetle is found among vegetables at a shop in New Cumnock, Strathclyde. New Moon
Saturday *March 3*	Sixty-five men, 10 women and 1,100 Huskies set out on the Iditarod, the annual 1,689km sledge race in Alaska.
Sunday *March 4*	Princess Anne attends the 4th Children's Royal Variety Performance in aid of the NSPCC at Her Majesty's Theatre, London.
Monday *March 5*	The European rocket Ariane is launched on its 8th flight. It carries the largest communications satellite ever—the 1.8 tonne Intelsat 5, which can handle 12,000 telephone calls and 2 colour TV channels at the same time!
Tuesday *March 6*	Pancake Day! A 48-tonne steel flask, used to transport nuclear waste, is tested by dropping it more than 9m down an old quarry near Cheddar Gorge in Somerset.
Wednesday *March 7*	A new Bubble Car, the Bamby, is launched at the Ideal Home Exhibition in London: top speed 56kph!
Thursday *March 8*	370,000,000 children in China have each been asked to give one fen (about a farthing) to help save the Giant Pandas from starvation.
Friday *March 9*	Prince Edward is sent a Gorillagram to wish him an early Happy Birthday! He'll be 19 tomorrow.
Saturday *March 10*	Invasion of octopuses on the Dorset coast: one fisherman has caught 8! A street in West Berlin is named after Jesse Owens, the great American athlete, who won 4 gold medals at the 1936 Berlin Olympics.
Sunday *March 11*	Sponsored crawl in Cambridge in aid of the Save the Children Fund — 3.2km from King's Parade to Grantchester. All Change at Welney Nature Reserve in Norfolk! 500 swans, who have wintered there, leave for Siberia in the morning and another 500 arrive in the afternoon — also on their way north to Siberia.
Monday *March 12*	The Pocket Money Monitor is published today. A nationwide miners' strike begins.
Tuesday *March 13*	Budget Day: VAT on fish and chips (and all take-away food). Prices will go up by 15% from May 1!

Wednesday *March 14*	Commonwealth Day. The West Wales Naturalists' Trust is going to put wooden puffins on the cliffs on Cardigan Island to try to lure real puffins back.
Thursday *March 15*	Julius Caesar was assassinated in Rome in 44BC. Thieves escape with silver worth £5,000,000 from Woburn Abbey in Bedfordshire.
Friday *March 16*	Britain's first safari park, at Longleat in Wiltshire, is 18 years old today! Fires in Ashdown Forest, Sussex
Saturday *March 17*	St Patrick's Day. The University Boat Race is postponed less than an hour before it is due to start, after the Cambridge boat collides with a barge. New Moon
Sunday *March 18*	Oxford wins the 130th University Boat Race in a record time of 16 mins 45 secs.
Monday *March 19*	The York Helmet, which was found 2 years ago on a building site, goes on display at the Castle Museum.
Tuesday *March 20*	Newcastle Disease, a dangerous form of fowl pest, breaks out at Exmouth, Devon. It's the 7th outbreak in Britain in 3 weeks!
Wednesday *March 21*	A Soviet nuclear-powered submarine collides with a US aircraft carrier in the Sea of Japan. Project Papillon, to breed butterflies, is born on Guernsey.
Thursday *March 22*	A minute's silence for peace round the world. Ban on Italian parsley from midnight after the discovery of 70 live colorado beetles in the last 2 weeks: 40 in Scotland and 30 in England.
Friday *March 23*	A cyclone flattens the town of Borrollola in N. Australia. Wettest day of the year so far
Saturday *March 24*	Athlete Zola Budd (17) arrives in Britain from South Africa. £21,800,000 is taken from a security vault on the outskirts of Rome—the biggest single theft ever in Italy!
Sunday *March 25*	British Summer Time Begins at 1am GMT. The first Milk Cup (which began life as the League Cup) to be held on a Sunday at Wembley ends in a goalless draw between Everton and Liverpool.
Monday *March 26*	Zola Budd, the South African athlete, applies for a British passport at the Immigration Office in Croydon: it would mean she could run for Britain in the Olympics this summer.

March

Named after the Roman god Mars. It has also been known as 'rough month', 'lengthening month', 'boisterous month' and 'windy month'.

The Pocket Money Monitor

The Pocket Money Monitor, an annual survey carried out by Gallup for Wall's Ice Cream, shows that children between the ages of 5 and 16 have had a cut of 14% in their pocket money during the last year! Although it varies slightly, according to where you live and whether you are a girl or boy, the average pocket money is now £1.05, compared with £1.22 last year.

Pocket Money Table

Year	Total	Boys	Girls	5–7 yrs	8–10 yrs	11–13 yrs	14–16 yrs
1980	99p	99p	99p	59p	66p	109p	151.5p
1981	113p	117p	108p	55p	87p	132p	173p
1982	94.5p	93p	95.5p	64p	74p	113.5p	128p
1983	122p	124p	115p	90p	103p	141p	178p
1984	105p	101p	109p	42p	73p	113p	187p

March 6:
The Post Office issues 5 new stamps called British Cattle

26ᴾ — Hereford Bull

16ᴾ — Highland Cow

28ᴾ — Welsh Black Bull

20½ᴾ — Chillingham Wild Bull

31ᴾ — Irish Moiled Cow

PROJECT PAPILLON

Project Papillon, which was hatched on Guernsey this month, sends pupae all over Britain to help boost the butterfly population. They are bred in old, disused tomato greenhouses and cultivated on rough grass, nettles and nectar-rich plants. When they are ready, the pupae are picked off the leaves like fruit and put into warm, dry boxes ready for hatching or posting. The different species that Project Papillon breeds are Painted Ladies, Red Admirals, Speckled Woods and Small Tortoiseshells.

Tuesday *March 27*	*Starlight Express*, the roller-skating musical based on the stories by the Rev Awdrey, opens at the Apollo, Victoria.
Wednesday *March 28*	Liverpool beats Everton 1–0 in the Cup Final replay at Maine Rd, Manchester.
Thursday *March 29*	The last ½p coin leaves the Royal Mint today: it stops being legal tender at the end of the year.
Friday *March 30*	The first swallows of summer are seen at Bourton-on-the-Water, Gloucestershire and reported to the RSPB.
Saturday *March 31*	The Grand National is won by Hallo Dandy from Greystoke, Cumbria. William Hill, the bookmakers, offer 10–1 on the Princess of Wales having twins!

TOP TEN CHILDREN'S BOOKS 1984
(according to the Book Marketing Council's survey)

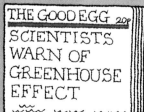

CHILDREN'S CHOICE

1) *The Beaver Book of Skool Verse* by Jennifer Curry
2) *The Big Book for Greedy Cooks* by Alison Leach and Deborah van der Beek
3) *Black Harvest* by Ann Cheetham
4) *Crazy Joke Book* by Janet Rogers
5) *Discovering Life on Earth* by David Attenborough
6) *Eric the Punk Cat* by Adrian Henri
7) *Fungus the Bogeyman* by Raymond Briggs
8) *Grange Hill Rules! OK?* by Robert Leeson
9) *Happy Families* by Allan Ahlberg
10) *Haunted House Pop-Up Book* by Jan Pienkowski

THE GOOD EGG 20p

SCIENTISTS WARN OF GREENHOUSE EFFECT

DAILY BLAH 19p

THE OLDEST DOG IN THE WORLD DIES, AGED 32, IN QUEENSLAND, AUSTRALIA

DAILY TRUMPET

BONES OF AN 80,000-YEAR-OLD WILD OX FOUND IN EAST LONDON

CHATTERBOX 25p

BRITISH TELEPHONE BOX FLIES TO U.S.A

UK FACT FILE 1984

Total area of the United Kingdom
244,099.7 square kilometres

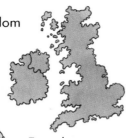

Capital City
London (157,9.9 square
kilometres: population
6,696,000)

Population of UK
55,776,000

Females
28,701,000

Males
27,064,000

Births
729,600

Marriages
395,800

Deaths
644,900

*Most popular boys' name   James   Elizabeth   *Most popular girls' name

Licensed vehicles
20,765,000

Driving tests
1,784,112 (50.93% fail)

Head of State
Queen Elizabeth II

Prime Minister
Margaret Hilda Thatcher

Astronomer Royal
Prof. Francis Graham Smith

Poet Laureate
Sir John Betjeman (until
May 19)
Ted Hughes

Olympic Year

Leap Year

* according to *The Times* newspaper

April

Sunday *April 1*	Mother's Day. Hayley Griffiths (7) and Jimmy Endicott (6), from Doncaster, win the Bisto Kids of the Year title. Henry Weston, from Hampshire, and Robin Cross, from Norwich, set off from Tower Bridge in London to run round the world. New Moon
Monday *April 2*	Hans Christian Andersen was born at Odense in Denmark in 1805. The first osprey arrives back at Loch Garten on Spey-side after wintering in the Gambia, West Africa.
Tuesday *April 3*	India's first spaceman is launched, with two Soviet cosmonauts, in a Soyuz 11 space capsule from central Asia.
Wednesday *April 4*	Soyuz 11 docks with Salyut-7, the orbiting space station. The QE2 collides with a jetty in Gibraltar.
Thursday *April 5*	Princess Diana visits the Royal Doulton factory in Stoke-on-Trent: she helps to make a china figure of Little Boy Blue, and is given a 'Bunnykins' mug and plate for Prince William.
Friday *April 6*	The US space shuttle Challenger, with a 5-man crew on board, lifts off from Cape Canaveral, Florida. Zola Budd, the South African athlete, is granted British citizenship.
Saturday *April 7*	Dial 010-1-900 410-6272 and listen to the shuttle astronauts talking to Mission Control. Three minutes at the cheap rate cost £1.62!
Sunday *April 8*	US astronaut George Nelson walks more than 60m in space with a rocket-powered back-pack and tries to steady Solar Max, a satellite which has been malfunctioning for 3 years.
Monday *April 9*	A 6.7m high granite memorial stone leaves Retford, Nottinghamshire, for Port Stanley in the Falklands.
Tuesday *April 10*	The Post Office issues four new stamps marking the opening of the International Garden Festival, Liverpool, and the 150th anniversary of the Royal Institute of British Architects.
Wednesday *April 11*	Australia replaces *God Save The Queen* with *Advance Australia Fair* as their National Anthem. US astronauts successfully replace a control box in the Solar Max satellite.
Thursday *April 12*	Cop of the Month award for bravery in New York goes to a 1.2m high, one-armed robot called *RM13*!
Friday *April 13*	So far, nearly 100 Great Crested Newts (a protected species) have been saved from a pond at Broughton, Northamptonshire, which is going to be filled in for building works!

April

The opening month – from the Latin 'aperire', which means to open. Also known as the time of budding.

APRIL RECORD BOARD

Peter Davies, from Blackpool, sets a new world distance record for flying a microlight aircraft: he flies 547km from Suffolk to Land's End—almost doubling the previous record!

The French catamaran Jet Services crosses the Atlantic from New York to the Lizard in Cornwall in 8 days 16 hours 33 mins, smashing the record for the 4988km journey set in 1981 by 17 hours 33 mins!

Ann Ferris becomes the first woman jockey to win the Irish Grand National.

Mark Ryder, from Quedgeley, Gloucestershire, eats 1000 grey elvers (baby eels) in 27 secs, knocking 2 secs off his previous world best!

The first stilt sandpiper to be seen in Britain for 8 years is spotted at Frodsham in Cheshire.

April 25
ANZAC stands for Australia and New Zealand Army Corps.
ANZAC Day marks the anniversary of the landing on the Gallipoli Peninsula in Turkey during World War I.

April 10th
The Post Office issues 4 new stamps to mark the opening of the International Gardens Festival in Liverpool and the 150th anniversary of the Royal Institute of British Architects and the Chartered Institute of Building:

16ᵖ URBAN RENEWAL – LIVERPOOL

20½ᵖ URBAN RENEWAL – DURHAM

28ᵖ URBAN RENEWAL – BRISTOL

31ᵖ URBAN RENEWAL – PERTH

A RECIPE

The Royal Institute of British Architects' 150th Birthday Cake was so big that it took 6½ hours to bake! Among the ingredients were 49.9kg of cake mix, 15.9kg of marzipan, 5.4kg of royal icing and 18.2kg of caramel.

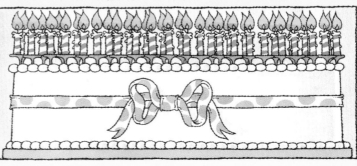

Saturday *April 14*	Zola Budd, the 17-year-old athlete from South Africa, wins her first race in England, the 3,000m at Dartford, Kent, in 9mins 2.6secs.
Sunday *April 15*	An earth tremor, measuring 3.3 on the Richter Scale, shakes over 500 sq km of Wales bounded by Newton, Llandrindod Wells and Knighton, South Wales. New Moon
Monday *April 16*	Two pairs of white-winged wood duck from the Wildfowl Trust at Slimbridge in Gloucestershire fly back to Thailand on a British Airways plane.
Tuesday *April 17*	For the first time, swallows are using the 5.6km Great St Bernard Road Tunnel on their way north from Italy to Switzerland. They've only used it going south in the autumn before!
Wednesday *April 18*	Two Britons parachute 304.8m from the 3rd stage of the Eiffel Tower in Paris.
Thursday *April 19*	The Queen distributes the Royal Maundy at the Maundy Service in Southwell Minster, Nottinghamshire. The Aldershot Military Museum opens—complete with telescopic beds.
Friday *April 20*	Good Friday. Hot Cross Bun Ceremonies at St Bartholomew the Great, Smithfield, London, at noon. The conservatory on top of the Barbican Centre in London opens today—120 species of plants and 2 fishponds.
Saturday *April 21*	The Queen's birthday. Police ban visits to the pyramids in Egypt: a strange gas is leaking from one of the pharaoh's tombs.
Sunday *April 22*	Easter Sunday. Holy Year ends when the Pope closes the Holy Door at St Peter's Basilica in Rome. It will not be opened again until the next Holy Year in 1999.
Monday *April 23*	Bank Holiday. St George's Day. The Leaning Tower of Pisa trembles during a series of earth tremors on the west coast of Italy. Sunniest Easter holiday for 35 years
Tuesday *April 24*	Skyscrapers sway in San Francisco during a powerful earthquake that measures at least 6 on the Richter Scale. The city was devastated by an earthquake 78 years ago.
Wednesday *April 25*	ANZAC Day: war veterans in Australia refuse to sing their new national anthem *Advance Australia Fair* and stick to *God Save the Queen* at special ANZAC Day services.

Thursday April 26	A giant conger eel, weighing more than 38kg, is caught at Southbourne, near Christchurch in Dorset.
Friday April 27	The Coast-to-Coast Footpath across southern Scotland, from Portpatrick in Wigtownshire to Cockburnspath in Berwickshire, is opened today.
Saturday April 28	Huge forest and moorland fires because of the hot, dry, sunny weather. Dartmoor has been devastated—also large areas of N Wales and the Peak District.
Sunday April 29	On view for one day only, the rare Snake Head Fritillary (a member of the lily family) at the Suffolk Trust for Nature Conservation's reserve at Framsden. Two Soviet cosmonauts make their 3rd space walk in a week!
Monday April 30	The Royal Institute of British Architects is 150 years old this year: they celebrate with a special Festival of Architecture and a huge cake which weighs more than 90kg and is decorated with 150 candles!

TOP TEN NAMES 1984
(according to Mr and Mrs Brown in *The Times* correspondence column)

Girls
1) Elizabeth (1)
2) Louise (2)
3) Charlotte (5)
4) Victoria (6)
5) Jane (3)
6) Sarah (7)
7) Mary (4)
8) Alexandra (10)
9) Katherine (9)
10) Emily (10)

Boys
1) James (1)
2) William (2)
3) Edward (3)
4) Thomas (5)
5) John (7)
6) Alexander (4)
7) Charles (6)
8) David (8)
9) Nicholas (10)
10) Richard (9)

The figures in brackets show the positions last year.

DAILY BLURB 21p
FORGED £50 NOTES FLOOD THE COUNTRY
£50

THE HOOT 20p
SCIENTISTS EXAMINE A CRICKET-BALL SIZED METEORITE WHICH LANDED IN WOLVERHAMPTON

DAILY MOON 16p
BOMB EXPLODES AT TERMINAL 2 AT HEATHROW AIRPORT — 22 INJURED

The Frog 19p
HEDGEHOG CRISPS LAUNCHED

May

Tuesday May 1

A plague of browntail caterpillars in hawthorn and mountain ash trees in Portsmouth! They can cause itches and rashes.

New Moon

Wednesday May 2

The Queen opens the International Garden Festival in Liverpool. A black rhino called Parky (after Michael Parkinson) arrives at Chester Zoo from Whipsnade Park.

Thursday May 3

Timothy Severin and a team of international rowers set off from Greece to retrace the voyage of Jason and the Argonauts in their quest for the Golden Fleece.

Friday May 4

A farmer has discovered a hoard of medieval gold coins in a field near Sturminster Newton, Dorset. They are nobles, half-nobles and quarter nobles, dating from the reigns of Edward III to Henry VI.

Saturday May 5

A baby dolphin is born, tail first, at Whipsnade Park.

Sunday May 6

5000 people challenge the world record for musical chairs at Woking, Surrey. Zola Budd sets a world record for a teenager in a 10km road race in Oslo: her time is 31mins 42secs.

Monday May 7

Bank Holiday. The Olympic torch is lit from the flame at Olympia, in Greece, and starts its journey to Los Angeles, USA, for the Games this summer. It is taken by helicopter to Athens and will fly from there to New York!

Tuesday May 8

The Queen officially opens the £480,000,000 Thames Flood Barrier. More than 2000 balloons are released to celebrate!

Wednesday May 9

Hugh King-Fretts (36), from Devon, ends his 4183km row across the Atlantic from Tenerife to Barbados. He has to swim the last 500m after being thrown from his 9m boat *Hulu* by a giant wave.

Thursday May 10

Six Nile crocodiles swim at the Commonwealth Institute in London, as part of the Great Zimbabwe Exhibition.

Friday May 11

20,000 people are homeless in central Italy after the third earthquake (measuring 4.9 on the Richter Scale) in a fortnight.

Saturday May 12

Beginning of National Bike Week.

Sunday May 13

20,142 runners take part in the London Marathon. Charles Spedding (31), of Durham, wins in 2hrs 9mins 57secs and Ingrid Kristiansen breaks last year's record with 2hrs 24mins 26secs.

May

Takes its name from Maia, the goddess of growth and increase, or from 'maiores', the Latin word for elders, who were honoured this month. The Anglo Saxons called it 'thrimilce' because cows could be milked three times a day now. An old Dutch name was 'bloumaand' which means blossoming month.

The Jorvik Viking Centre

The Jorvik Viking Centre, which opens in York this month, takes you back in time 1000 years to find out just what life was really like in a Viking settlement—complete with sounds and smells! You travel in a special time capsule, the sounds are on a 64-channel track and the smells (including putrid fish and rotting apples) are provided by special tablets. The Centre is built on the site of an important excavation made by the York Archeological Trust in Coppergate between 1976 and 1981. Viking houses and workshops were unearthed and, altogether, 35,000 different finds were made—from coins to fleas!

ZARA AND CO.

In the dictionary it says that giraffes are remarkable for their long necks and legs, not to mention their spotted skins. Perhaps this is why, at London Zoo, they are named after famous sportswomen and men. Zara (born on May 25) is named after Zara Long, the Olympic swimmer. She joins Virginia, who was born in 1968, and was named after Virginia Wade, the tennis player. Hilary, born in 1975, was named after Sir Edmund Hilary, the explorer, and Dawn, born in 1978, after Dawn Frazer, another famous Olympic swimmer.

MAP OF THE OLYMPIC FLAME'S JOURNEY FROM GREECE TO LOS ANGELES

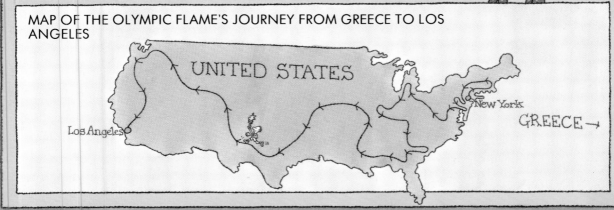

UNITED STATES

Los Angeles

New York

GREECE →

Monday *May 14*	Forest fires at Thetford, Norfolk, have destroyed thousands of trees.
Tuesday *May 15*	The Post Office issues new stamps to mark the 25th anniversary of CEPT and the second European Parliamentary Elections. David Hempleman-Adams becomes the first man to walk over 400km alone across the Arctic to the magnetic North Pole. New Moon
Wednesday *May 16*	Sixty-five people are hurt when a train crashes into the buffers of Liverpool Street Station in London.
Thursday *May 17*	The Prince of Wales opens the new Jorvik Viking Centre in York. A horse gives birth to a zebra colt at Louisville Zoo in Kentucky.
Friday *May 18*	Sheep herding demonstration in Paternoster Square by St Paul's Cathedral in London.
Saturday *May 19*	The FA Cup Final at Wembley: Everton beats Watford 2–0. The Poet Laureate, Sir John Betjeman, dies aged 77.
Sunday *May 20*	The statue of Nelson is being cleaned — 44.2m above Trafalgar Square in London.
Monday *May 21*	New roses at the Chelsea Flower Show include Selfridge, to celebrate the famous shop's 75th birthday, and Avocet, in honour of the RSPB (their symbol is an avocet).
Tuesday *May 22*	About 125,000 children are sent home from school because of a strike by two of the main teachers' unions.
Wednesday *May 23*	The European rocket Ariane is launched and puts a US communications satellite into orbit.
Thursday *May 24*	A pair of peregrine falcons are nesting at Symonds Yat in the Wye Valley—the first for 30 years!
Friday *May 25*	Terminal 4 at Heathrow airport is 'topped out' by the Secretary of State for Transport, Nicholas Ridley. A baby giraffe called Zara is born at London Zoo.
Saturday *May 26*	A collared fly catcher is sighted at North Down Park, Margate. The first Trans-Pennine Canal Marathon, on the Leeds and Liverpool Canal, starts today in Leeds.
Sunday *May 27*	International Paper Darts Flying Championships at Bracknell, Berkshire, 10am – 6pm. Miss Margaret Harris, from Southampton, wins *Mastermind 1984* with the highest score ever recorded.

Monday *May 28*	Bank Holiday. Zola Budd becomes the British 1,500m champion at Cwmbran in Wales in 4min 4.39secs. Coldest and wettest Spring Bank Holiday for more than 40 years
Tuesday *May 29*	The Prince of Wales describes a proposed extension to the National Gallery in London as being 'like a monstrous carbuncle on the face of a much-loved friend'.
Wednesday *May 30*	A partial eclipse of the sun can be seen in Britain from 6.14pm to sunset. Earth tremors in Leicestershire, Nottinghamshire and parts of Lincolnshire measure 2.7 on the Richter Scale. New Moon — the second of the month!
Thursday *May 31*	Last journey across the Clyde for the Renfrew vehicle ferry — from Clydebank to Renfrew. Angry Welsh farmers block the roads into Aberystwyth with tractors and Land Rovers to disrupt the Milk Bicycle Race in protest at EEC cuts in milk quotas.

The Happy Birthday Page!

Worcester Cathedral is 900
The Royal College of Arms is 500
The Royal Highland and Agricultural Society of Scotland is 200
The Royal Institute of British Architects is 150
The National Society for the Prevention of Cruelty to Children is 100
The Highland Cattle Society is 100
Part I of the Oxford English Dictionary (A to ANT) is 100
The Greenwich Meridian is 100
Greenwich Mean Time is 100
Women's tennis at Wimbledon is 100
The Manchester Ship Canal is 90
Donald Duck is 50
The National Maritime Museum is 50
The British Council is 50
D-Day is 40
NATO is 35
The Bash Street Kids are 30
The Mini is 25
Prince William is 2

June

Friday *June 1*	Robert Dover's Games at Chipping Campden in Gloucestershire include tug-of-war, shin kicking and climbing the greasy pole!
Saturday *June 2*	Ninety yachts leave Plymouth for Newport, Rhode Island, at the start of the Trans-Atlantic Single-Handed Race.
Sunday *June 3*	A new D-Day Museum is opened in Portsmouth by the Queen Mother. Michael Cudahy breaks the Pennine Way record: he runs 436km in 2 days 21hrs 54mins 30secs!
Monday *June 4*	New Orchid Wardens have been appointed in Buckinghamshire, Cambridgeshire, Kent and Yorkshire, to protect precious rare orchids.
Tuesday *June 5*	The Post Office issues a special stamp to mark the Economic Summit Conference in London.
Wednesday *June 6*	Fortieth anniversary celebrations of the D-Day landings in France at the end of World War II. Zola Budd wins the 3,000m at Crystal Palace, London, in 8 mins 40.22 secs.
Thursday *June 7*	Striking miners go to the House of Commons: more than 120 people are arrested, including an MP, after fighting in Parliament Square.
Friday *June 8*	Mrs Nancy Reagan visits London Zoo and meets her namesake Nancy, a 2-week-old reindeer.
Saturday *June 9*	Happy Birthday Donald Duck — 50 today! Oleg Czougeda (20) of the Soviet Union wins the final stage of the longest cycle race in Britain—the 1770km Milk Race—in Blackpool.
Sunday *June 10*	Whit Sunday. More than 40 children collapse from heat stroke during a marching bands concert at Cotmanhay in Derbyshire.
Monday *June 11*	The Princess of Wales goes to the premiere of the film *Indiana Jones and the Temple of Doom* and meets one of the actors—12-year-old Ke Huy Quan!
Tuesday *June 12*	Monks Hill in Weston-super-Mare is the stickiest place in the south west after gallons of treacle spill from a tanker. The M1 is blocked for 40 minutes at Sandiacre, Derbyshire, by 3 tonnes of fruit and vegetables.
Wednesday *June 13*	The 2900-tonne navy frigate *Jupiter* crashes into London Bridge while doing a 'U' turn in the river Thames. Full Moon

June

Takes its name from the great goddess Juno, or from 'juniores', the Latin word for young people, who were honoured this month. The old Dutch name was 'Zomer-maand', which means summer month. The old Saxon name was 'Sere-moneth', which means dry month.

(June 26) Meridian Day: it is 100 years since a line running through the Greenwich Observatory was adopted as the universal meridian, 0° longitude. It is also 100 years since Greenwich Mean Time was adopted as universal time. Celebrations are held in Greenwich Park and the RAF Falcons parachute team drop in!

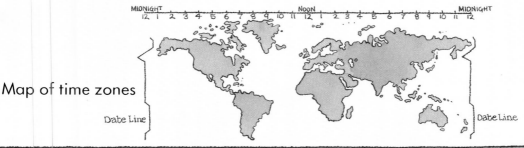

Map of time zones

Date Line   Date Line

June 4th
The rare orchids that need protecting are:
The monkey orchid
The military orchid
The coral root orchid
The early spider orchid

DAILY BUBBLE 20p

O'LEVELS AND CSE'S TO BE REPLACED BY GCSE

FRED'S NEWS

FIRST VIRGIN ATLANTIC FLIGHT TO NEW YORK FROM GATWICK— £99 SINGLE

The Grapevine

EUROPEAN PARLIAMENTARY ELECTIONS

25p

FORTISSIMO

INDIAN TROOPS STORM SIKH SHRINE THE GOLDEN TEMPLE OF AMRITSAR

Thursday *June 14*	The Guinness World of Records Exhibition opens in London.
Friday *June 15*	The last chimney, more than 106m tall is demolished, at the British Steel Corporation's site at Corby, Northamptonshire, which closed 4 years ago.
Saturday *June 16*	The Queen's Official Birthday. She rides her horse *Burmese* at the Trooping the Colour, where more than 1600 officers and men are on parade. There's a 41-gun salute from Hyde Park and a flypast over Buckingham Palace by 9 RAF Tornadoes.
Sunday *June 17*	Hot air balloon races at Leeds Castle in Kent to commemorate the 200th anniversary of the first British manned balloon flight by Vincent Lunardi.
Monday *June 18*	A plaque in Plymouth which lists the Pilgrim Fathers who sailed to America on the *Mayflower* in 1620 is replaced by one which names the Pilgrim Mothers as well.
Tuesday *June 19*	Rory McCarthy, from London, sets a new world hang-gliding record: he is released from a hot-air balloon at 10515.6m and lands safely near Diss, Norfolk.
Wednesday *June 20*	Floods in the east! Pedestrians are knocked off their feet by the rain in Essex, Suffolk and Norfolk. Motorists abandon their cars in Colchester and tents are swept away from a camp site near Ipswich.
Thursday *June 21*	Longest day of the year: Druids perform a ritual summer ceremony at Stonehenge. Prince William of Wales is two today!
Friday *June 22*	Princess Margaret plays herself (for one minute) in BBC Radio's *The Archers*.
Saturday *June 23*	Two penny-farthing bicycles set out from Land's End in Cornwall for John O'Groats in Scotland to raise money for the NSPCC.
Sunday *June 24*	Midsummer Day. Twelve thousand people take part in the London to Brighton Bicycle Race in aid of the British Heart Foundation. Michael Willis (29), a guard on London Underground, scores a record 1682 points in 3 games and becomes the new National Scrabble Champion.
Monday *June 25*	The first launch of the new American space shuttle Discovery is postponed 30 mins before lift-off — a computer fault.

Tuesday *June 26*	The Post Office issues 4 new stamps to celebrate the centenary of the Greenwich Meridian. The American space shuttle Discovery's launch is delayed again—4 secs before lift-off!
Wednesday *June 27*	The hot, dry weather continues: Penzance in Cornwall has only 3.6mm of rain during the whole month! Adder warnings in West Sussex!
Thursday *June 28*	The World Wildlife Fund announces that the first Large Blue butterfly has been seen in the West Country since it officially became extinct in 1979.
Friday *June 29*	Wanted for £37 a day: elves to help Father Christmas in a new film called *Santa Claus the Movie*! New Moon
Saturday *June 30*	The new A303 relief road near Montacute and Stoke-sub-Hamden in Somerset is opened today—complete with special badger tunnels.

June 26th
The Post Office issues 4 new stamps to celebrate the centenary of the Greenwich Meridian:

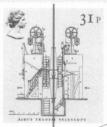

16ᴾ GREENWICH 1884 - MERIDIAN - 1984

20½ᴾ GREENWICH 1884 - MERIDIAN - 1984

28ᴾ GREENWICH 1884 - MERIDIAN - 1984

31ᴾ AIRY'S TRANSIT TELESCOPE GREENWICH 1884 - MERIDIAN - 1984

DAILY WHIZ 18ᴾ	RIGHT HO! 20ᴾ	CLANGER 22ᴾ	DAILY OWL 19ᴾ
BRITISH SHIP MARQUES SINKS OFF BERMUDA IN THE TALL SHIPS RACE – 19 MISSING	RECORD EXPORTS OF CHRISTMAS PUDDINGS	40,000,000 YEAR-OLD FOSSIL PALM TREE FOUND IN THE ARCTIC	CAT SURVIVES FALL OF NEARLY 55m FROM A NEW YORK SKY-SCRAPER WITH A FEW CUTS AND BRUISES

LOST AND FOUND IN THE LAST YEAR
(on Southern Region trains and stations)

50 sets of false teeth
7000 carrier bags
16,000 umbrellas
4000 gloves

July

Sunday *July 1*	Happy 22nd Birthday to the Princess of Wales! Nick Sanders, from Glossop, Derbyshire, arrives back at Blackpool Tower and breaks the record for cycling round the coast of Britain: he travelled 8849.5km in 22 days 4hrs.
Monday *July 2*	A replica of the *Golden Hind*, the boat in which Sir Francis Drake sailed round the world between 1577 and 1580, arrives at Manchester docks.
Tuesday *July 3*	The annual report says that the Leaning Tower of Pisa has moved by 0.4mm in the past year!
Wednesday *July 4*	Independence Day, USA. The government announced that national dog licences are going to be abolished.
Thursday *July 5*	The Statue of Liberty in New York Harbour loses her torch: it's taken off by a huge crane as part of her face-lift.
Friday *July 6*	Three otters, bred at the Otter Trust in Suffolk, are released into the wild to help to increase the otter population of East Anglia. It's so hot that the M40's westbound carriageway at Stokenchurch, Buckinghamshire, cracks.
Saturday *July 7*	Lyndon Dunsby (16), from Dover, swims the Channel in a record 8hrs 34mins—18mins faster than the record set in 1982. Michael Reid (43), from Ipswich, swims the Channel for the 30th time!
Sunday *July 8*	John McEnroe wins the Men's Singles title at Wimbledon, beating Jimmy Connors 6-1, 6-1, 6-2.
Monday *July 9*	York Minster is struck by lightning—the roof of the south transept is destroyed by fire. Smoking is banned on all London tube trains from today!
Tuesday *July 10*	Tim Batstone (25), who left Southend Pier on May 2, finishes windsurfing round the coast of Britain (3218km) to raise money for lifeboat stations.
Wednesday *July 11*	Lightning strikes the pitch and stops play in the Minor Counties Cricket Match between Staffordshire and Norfolk at Brewood near Wolverhampton.
Thursday *July 12*	The Queen Mother attends the topping out ceremony at the new Lloyd's Building in London. A time capsule, sealed in the roof, includes a newspaper and a quill pen!

July

Named in honour of Julius Caesar. The old Dutch name was 'Hooy-maand' — hay month and the old Saxon name was 'Maedd-monath' because the cattle were turned into the meadow to feed.

WELCOME TO THE LOS ANGELES OLYMPICS!

The Olympic flame arrives from Greece and is carried into the stadium by Gina Hemphill, who is the grand-daughter of the great US athlete, Jesse Owens. 3,636 relay runners have brought it 15,000km across America from New York. After the official opening ceremony, a 1000-voice choir sings WELCOME, and an 800-piece band and 84 grand pianos play. A Rocket Man with WELCOME on his back flies down and lands in the stadium and five airplanes write WELCOME in huge letters in the sky!

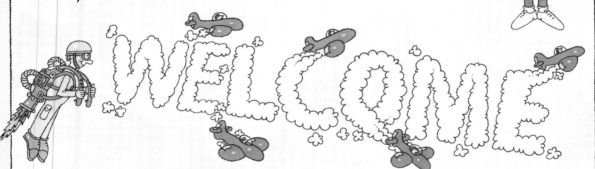

July 31st
The Post Office issues 5 new stamps to mark the 200th anniversary of the first mail coach from Bath & Bristol to London

AN *Attack on the* EXETER Mail *in 1816*   16P

THE NORWICH Mail *in a Thunder Storm 1827*   16P

THE EDINBURGH Mail *Snowbound in 1831*   16P

THE *Original* BATH Mail Coach *of 1784*   16P

THE HOLYHEAD & LIVERPOOL Mails *1828*   16P

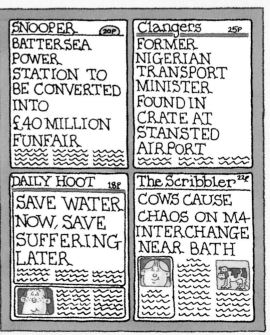

SNOOPER 20P
BATTERSEA POWER STATION TO BE CONVERTED INTO £40 MILLION FUNFAIR

Clangers 25P
FORMER NIGERIAN TRANSPORT MINISTER FOUND IN CRATE AT STANSTED AIRPORT

DAILY HOOT 18P
SAVE WATER NOW, SAVE SUFFERING LATER

The Scribbler 22P
COWS CAUSE CHAOS ON M4 INTERCHANGE NEAR BATH

Friday *July 13*	Zola Budd breaks the women's 2000m record at Crystal Palace in London with a time of 5min 33.15secs. Derek Fowler (52), from Surrey, sets out from Kitty Hawk, North Carolina, to fly a microlight 4376km across America to Lake Elsinore in California. Full Moon
Saturday *July 14*	St Swithin's Day. Round Britain Powerboat Race starts from Southsea Castle, Portsmouth 10am.
Sunday *July 15*	Competitors sweep for buried treasure in the first Metal Detection Rally at Newbury in Berkshire.
Monday *July 16*	The City of London Festival. The Pope goes ski-ing in the Italian Alps.
Tuesday *July 17*	A Soviet spacecraft, Soyuz T12 with a new crew of 3 including 1 woman, is launched to link up with the orbiting space station, Salyut-7. A fly stows away on board.
Wednesday *July 18*	French Channel ports are blockaded by lorry drivers in protest at the dock strike in Britain. Nearly 200 lorry drivers are stranded on the M21 near Folkestone because of the dock strike and the blockade of French ports.
Thursday *July 19*	The skeleton of a sailor from the *Mary Rose* is buried at Portsmouth Cathedral—439 years exactly from the day he and 700 others died.
Friday *July 20*	High Court ban on chocolate, fruit, rose and sausage-smelling erasers!
Saturday *July 21*	Osma Momtaz (24), from Cairo, sets a new record for swimming both ways across the Channel in 21hours 3mins.
Sunday *July 22*	Vandals saw the right arm off the statue of Hans Christian Andersen's Little Mermaid in Copenhagen harbour. The 7th World Wheelchair Games (Paralympics) at Stoke Mandeville Hospital in Buckinghamshire.
Monday *July 23*	Tim Severin and his modern-day *Argo* arrive in Soviet Georgia and prove that it is possible to cross the Bosphorus in a 20-oar boat with a square sail.
Tuesday *July 24*	The Princess of Wales carries out her last public engagement before the birth of her second baby: she opens a research centre at King's College Hospital, London.

Wednesday July 25	Soviet cosmonaut, Svetlana Savitskaya, becomes the 1st woman to walk in space: she leaves Salyut-7 for 3hrs 35mins and does some welding on the outside of the spacecraft. Jenny Currans (3), from West London, wins the 36th Miss Pears title. Whirlwind in Bramham, Yorkshire.
Thursday July 26	Happy Birthday Mick Jagger—41 today! Hailstones as big as golf balls pile up 25cm deep in Germany!
Friday July 27	Strong earth tremor in North Wales—buildings shake in Blaenau Ffestiniog, Portmadoc in Gwynedd, and on the Lleyn Peninsula. *Star Trek III – The Search for Spock* opens in London.
Saturday July 28	It has been so dry in Wales and the West Country—for nearly 7 weeks—that nearly 21,000,000 people are now affected. Lundy Island has imported a special soap that lathers in the sea, as no baths are allowed! New Moon
Sunday July 29	President Reagan opens the 23rd Olympic Games in Los Angeles. There is the 3rd earth tremor in 11 days in North Wales.
Monday July 30	The last four days of the month are very hot—with temperatures up to 30°C in south-east England and the Channel Isles.
Tuesday July 31	The Post Office issues five new stamps to mark the Bicentenary of the first Mail Coach run from Bath and Bristol to London. Twin jaguar cubs, called Claire and Richard, are born at London Zoo.

TOP TEN TOYS 1984
(according to Toys International)

1) Masters of the Universe (Mattel)
2) A-Team figures and vehicles (Rainbow Ertl)
3) Transformers (Hasbro)
4) Lego
5) My Little Pony (Hasbro)
6) A La Carte Kitchens (Bluebird)
7) Barbie (Mattel)
8) Robo Machines (Bandai)
9) Fisher Price Baby Dolls
10) Care Bears (Palitoy)
    Flower Fairies (Hornby)

TOP TEN BIRDS
(according to the British Trust for Ornithology)

1) Starling
2) House sparrow
3) Chaffinch
4) Blackbird
5) Wood pigeon
6) Robin
7) Blue tit
8) Wren
9) Willow warbler
10) Dunnock

August

Wednesday August 1

A new letter at the beginning of car number plates from today — B instead of A! A foot (complete with toe nails) is found in Lindow Moss, a peat bog near Wilmslow in Cheshire.

Thursday August 2

A whirlwind at Gotham, Nottinghamshire, uproots trees and lifts off roofs. The West Country has its heaviest rain for a month.

Friday August 3

No swimming in the River Thet at Thetford in Norfolk today after 8912 litres of concentrated orange juice spill into it from a lorry!

Saturday August 4

Happy 84th Birthday to Queen Elizabeth the Queen Mother! The European rocket Ariane is launched in French Guyana: it puts 2 telecommunications satellites into orbit.

Sunday August 5

Henry, an okapi, is born at London Zoo.

Monday August 6

Excavation Day at Lindow Moss: the body of a man is lifted out of the bog in a block of peat and driven to the mortuary at Macclesfield District General Hospital.

Tuesday August 7

The two Mersey tunnels are closed for the first time ever—as part of strike action by council workers. Two men are struck by lightning in Surrey.

Wednesday August 8

Mrs Thatcher meets herself at Madame Tussaud's in London: it's the 3rd version in 9 years! Soviet cosmonaut Svetlana Savitskaya celebrates her 36th birthday.

Thursday August 9

The Greater London Council celebrates its 21st birthday with a huge pink-and-white cake over 6m high and 12m wide outside the Festival Hall. The candles are 3m tall!

Friday August 10

The statue of Eros in Piccadilly Circus, London, is taken away to be repaired: his feathers are loose, his feet need seeing to and his bow needs straightening and restringing.

Saturday August 11

Sebastian Coe wins the gold medal and Steve Cram wins silver in the 1500m at the Los Angeles Olympics. Full Moon

Sunday August 17

The Perseid meteor shower is at its best today! International Birdman Rally at Bognor Regis, Sussex: Harald Zimmer becomes the first competitor ever to fly more than 50m off the end of the pier. He covers 57.8m and wins top prize.

Monday August 13

Thunderstorms in central Wales and south east England, a dust-devil on Jersey and a plague of snakes in Gloucester.

August

Named in honour of the Roman Emperor Augustus, whose lucky month it was. The old Dutch name was 'Oost-maand' — harvest month. The old Saxon name was 'Weodmonath' — weed month.

The Olympic Games

140 nations compete in the 23rd modern Olympic Games in Los Angeles although Communist countries, led by the Soviet Union, do not take part. Britain wins 5 gold, 10 silver and 22 bronze medals and comes fifth in the medals table. The USA comes top with 83 gold, 61 silver and 30 bronze.

Britain's Gold Medal Winners

Malcolm Cooper	Small Bore Rifle
Martin Cross	
Richard Budgett	
Andrew Holmes	Rowing – Coxed Fours
Steven Redgrave	
Adrian Ellison	
Tessa Sanderson	Javelin
Sebastian Coe	1500m
Daley Thompson	Decathlon

Gold medals are, in fact, made out of silver but are coated with 24-carat gold. They are worth about £170!

THE BLACKPOOL TOWER

The Blackpool Tower was opened in 1894. It is over 158m to the top of the flagpole and it takes 20 men all their time to keep it painted—as soon as it's finished, it's time to start again! From the top of the tower you can see as far as the Lake District and the Isle of Man AND you can post your cards which are specially franked 'Posted at the top of Blackpool Tower'!

ROUND-THE-WORLD-RUN

So far, Henry Weston and Robin Cross have worn out 7 pairs of running shoes each! They left London on April 1 and have run 5905km to Istanbul. From here their route crosses Syria, Saudi Arabia, Pakistan, India, Bangladesh, Australia and the USA.

Tuesday *August 14*	A submarine is caught in the nets of a 34-tonne fishing boat off Berry head, South Devon. Henry Weston and Robin Cross arrive in Istanbul, Turkey, at the end of the first stage of their round-the-world run.
Wednesday *August 15*	A new station on the Fairbourne miniature railway in Merioneth challenges the record for the longest place name in Britain: it's called GORSAFAWDDACHA'IDRAIGDDANHEDDOGLEDDOLL ONPENRHYNAREURDRAETHCEREDIGION!
Thursday *August 16*	Fourteen cyclists leave London at the start of a 14481km journey to India to raise money for Oxfam.
Friday *August 17*	Scientists report that Peat Bog Man, found earlier this month in Cheshire, is at least 1000 years old!
Saturday *August 18*	The Friendship '84 Games open in Lenin Stadium in Moscow for communist countries who boycotted the Los Angeles Olympics.
Sunday *August 19*	A lesser sandpiper—a rare small wading bird—is sighted at Dungeness, Kent. It probably drifted off course across the Atlantic while migrating from North to South America.
Monday *August 20*	The use of hosepipes is banned in NW England. The drought is still serious in the south west, Wales and Yorkshire.
Tuesday *August 21*	Peat Bog Man is taken in a special wooden box to London, to be examined by the British Museum. He is kept at 4°C in the mortuary of the Middlesex Hospital and given the name Pete Marsh.
Wednesday *August 22*	Miss Weston-super-Mare is crowned Miss United Kingdom. Miss Wrexham comes 2nd and Miss Northern Ireland 3rd.
Thursday *August 23*	A giant inflatable King Kong, 27m tall, stands on the roof of Blackpool Tower to help celebrate its 90th birthday!
Friday *August 24*	Mount Vesuvius erupted in AD 79, killing 200,000 people and destroying Pompeii and Herculaneum.
Saturday *August 25*	A 15m humpback whale is trapped in Loch Duich in Scotland for 24hrs before being freed by divers.
Sunday *August 26*	The Mini's 25th Birthday party is held at Donington racing circuit in Derbyshire and causes maximum traffic jam (of Minis) on the M1! New Moon

Monday *August 27*	Bank Holiday. A pleasure boat crashes into rocks near the Needles Lighthouse on the Isle of Wight: 55 people have to be rescued. Count down begins for the space shuttle Discovery.
Tuesday *August 28*	A fault is discovered and the launch of Discovery is postponed for 24 hours.
Wednesday *August 29*	Sefton, the cavalry horse who was badly injured 2 years ago when a bomb exploded in Hyde Park, leaves loose box no. 43 at the army barracks for the last time and retires to the Home of Rest for Horses in Buckinghamshire. 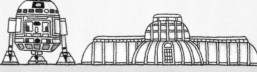
Thursday *August 30*	Supplies of blister kits, talcum powder and running shoes are flown out to Henry Weston and Robin Cross in Istanbul before they set out on the next stage of their round-the-world run.
Friday *August 31*	The British coaster *Polaris* (540 tonnes) hits Manacle Rocks off the Lizard Peninsula in Cornwall and 5 men are rescued.

IN In 1984

BMX bikes
Michael Jackson
Ewoks
SuperTed
Bob Geldof
International Teddy Bear Club
Couch Potatoes
Pete Marsh
Sam the Bald Eagle
British Telecom shares

OUT In 1984

The ½ pence coin
The £1 note
The Wombles
Star Wars figures and vehicles
Pete Marsh
Do They Know It's Christmas?
Smelly rubbers

ON THE MEND IN 1984

Blackpool Tower
Palm House, Kew
Statue of Liberty
Great Wall of China
Eros
Pete Marsh

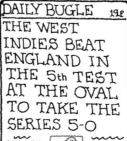

The Nosey Parker 20p

BMX (BICYCLE MOTO-CROSS) BIKES HIT BRITAIN

THE EAVESDROPPER 25p

UNEXPLODED WARTIME BOMB CLOSES M32 NEAR BRISTOL

DAILY BUGLE 19p

THE WEST INDIES BEAT ENGLAND IN THE 5th TEST AT THE OVAL TO TAKE THE SERIES 5-0

CHEEP 22p

CARL LEWIS (U.S.A) WINS 4 GOLD MEDALS AT LA OLYMPICS

September

Saturday
September 1

Ring 010-1-900-410-6272 and listen to the astronauts on space shuttle Discovery talking to mission control.

Sunday
September 2

Taxi Driver of the Year competition in Battersea Park, London. The Farnborough Air Show opens.

Monday
September 3

Postal charges go up: first class letters by 1p to 17p and second class by ½p to 13p.

Tuesday
September 4

Discovery's waste pipes are frozen up and the astronauts have to use a robot arm to knock off the ice!
The volcano Krafla erupts in Iceland.

Wednesday
September 5

Lisa Musgrave (9), from Mansfield, Nottinghamshire, wins the 1984 Brownie-Guide Tea Making Championship: she makes 658 cups and wins her own weight in tea!

Thursday
September 6

The 3 Soviet cosmonauts on board the orbiting space station Salyut-7 set a new endurance record of 212 days in space.

Friday
September 7

Plague of maggots in Gloucestershire! One of the highest and most active volcanoes in the world—Klyuchevskaya Sopka, (4850m), in the Soviet Union—erupts.

Saturday
September 8

The Quadrathon starts in Brighton with a 3.2km swim between Palace and West Piers, followed by a 48.2km walk to Tunbridge Wells.

Sunday
September 9

The Quadrathon carries on with a 160.9km cycle ride from Tunbridge Wells to Brands Hatch, followed by a full marathon (42.1km) to Gravesend in Kent. Steve Upton (27), from Rainham in Kent wins in 16hrs 8mins 8 secs!

Monday
September 10

Godstone is the best-kept large village in Surrey and its village hall is the best-kept village hall.   Full Moon

Tuesday
September 11

Widecombe Fair, near Newton Abbot in Devon: includes a pony show, sheep shearing, and pillow fighting on a slippery pole! Hurricane Diana hits the coast of Carolina in USA with winds up to 215kph.

Wednesday
September 12

After 6 months of drought, reservoirs are at record low levels and stand pipes are being put up in Yorkshire.

Thursday
September 13

An 11.5m long boat, believed to be over 2000 years old, is raised from a peat bog near Market Weighton in Humberside.

Friday *September 14*	Joe Kittinger (56), takes off from Maine, USA, in an attempt to become the first person to cross the Atlantic alone in a balloon!
Saturday *September 15*	Prince Harry (full name Henry Charles Albert David) is born at St Mary's Hospital, Paddington: he weighs 3.12kg.
Sunday *September 16*	The Reverend Wilbert Awdrey (73), who created *Thomas the Tank Engine* (and friends), shows how his model railway works at the Dean Forest Railway Preservation Society at Norchard in Gloucestershire.

September

This was the seventh month when the year used to start in March. The old Dutch name was 'Herst-maand'—autumn month. The old Saxon name was 'Gerst-monath'—barely month.

September 25th: Post office issue 4 new stamps for the 50th anniversary of the British Council

17ᴾ The British Council education for development

22ᴾ The British Council promoting the arts

31ᴾ The British Council technical training

34ᴾ The British Council language & libraries

DAILY WHOOP 20P
STRIKE AT DISNEYLAND

The Chuckle 16P
STARLINGS CAUSE HEALTH HAZARD IN WAKEFIELD

CRESCENDO 25P
PET REGISTER LAUNCHED IN LONDON

DAILY CHIRRUP
GREENHAM COMMON PEACE WOMEN EVICTED 22P

TOP TEN HISTORIC PROPERTIES AND GARDENS 1984
(according to the British Tourist Authority)

1) Tower of London (2,341,341 visitors)
2) Kew Gardens (1,084,291 visitors)
3) Roman Baths, Bath (931,169 visitors)
4) Edinburgh Castle (847,069 visitors)
5) Royal Botanic Gardens, Edinburgh (721,916 visitors)
6) Windsor Castle (717, 469 visitors)
7) Stonehenge (639,604 visitors)
8) Warwick Castle (563,996 visitors)
9) Shakespeare's birthplace, Stratford-upon-Avon (562,306 visitors)
10) Hampton Court (554,335 visitors)

Monday *September 17*	Scientists at the British Museum in London begin tests on Pete Marsh the Lindow Man (see Aug 1 and 6).
Tuesday *September 18*	Joe Kittinger, who has flown across the Atlantic from America alone in a balloon, crash lands in Italy and breaks a foot.
Wednesday *September 19*	Chay Blyth sets off in his 16.1m trimaran *Beefeater II* from New York to sail round Cape Horn to San Francisco. The record for the 23330.5km journey is 89 days 21 hrs.
Thursday *September 20*	A diver brings up 17th century pieces-of-eight from a wreck off the Isles of Scilly: three sunken ships were discovered 17 years ago and so far 30,000 silver coins have been recovered!
Friday *September 21*	Prince Harry is formally registered and given his National Health Insurance Number: LSCVT 275.
Saturday *September 22*	A baby pilot whale is stranded in Portland Harbour, Dorset.
Sunday *September 23*	Roy Blaikie (36), from Workington, Cumbria, wins the UK Bus Driver of the Year title in Blackpool.
Monday *September 24*	Pete Marsh, the Peat Bog Man, is taken from the mortuary at the Middlesex Hospital in London to a branch of the British Museum in Hackney to be examined.
Tuesday *September 25*	The National Exhibition of Children's Art opens at the Mall Galleries in London. New Moon
Wednesday *September 26*	The annual Clog and Apron Race at the Royal Botanic Gardens, Kew, 5.15pm.
Thursday *September 27*	The bodies of 2 British sailors, perfectly preserved in permafrost, have been found on Beechey Island in the North West Territories of Canada.
Friday *September 28*	Princess Anne appears on a coin for the first time! It's one of 4 crown coins issued to mark the 30th Commonwealth Parliamentary Conference, which opens today in Douglas, Isle of Man.
Saturday *September 29*	Operation Cleansweep is launched to clean up the New Forest this weekend. Horatio, Viscount Nelson was born in Norfolk, 1758.
Sunday *September 30*	Horseman's Sunday at Tattenham Corner, Epsom: more than 1000 horses, ponies, donkeys and goats attend a service and blessing 11.45am. Each animal gets a rosette.

October

Monday *October 1*	Annual procession of judges from Westminster Abbey to Parliament to mark the beginning of the legal year. Alderman Sir Alan Traill is elected the new Lord Mayor of London.
Tuesday *October 2*	Three Soviet cosmonauts return to earth from Salyut-7 after a record-breaking 238 days in space! A meteorite that looks like a hot black potato lands on a beach south of Perth, West Australia.
Wednesday *October 3*	A lizard measuring 91.4cm is caught in a garden at Ewell, Surrey. The telescope from Captain Scott's ship *Discovery* returns home after a trip through space on board the US shuttle Discovery!
Thursday *October 4*	Richard Marsh (13), from Durham, wins a Young Engineer for Britain Award with a machine made out of a toffee tin and two watering cans which turns the energy of sea waves into electricity.
Friday *October 5*	Hurricane Hortense just manages to reach south-east England, after sweeping across the West Indies. Wettest day of the year so far in London!
Saturday *October 6*	The latest idea to save Stonehenge from the wear and tear of hundreds of thousands of visitors each year is to build a second, synthetic, Stonehenge out of glass fibre and show that instead!
Sunday *October 7*	Pearly Kings and Queens, Princes and Princesses take part in the Pearly Harvest Festival at St Martin-in-the-Fields in London at 3pm.
Monday *October 8*	Annual Columbus Day parade down Fifth Avenue in New York. A new soft English cheese called Melbury, a relative of Lymeswold, is launched today.
Tuesday *October 9*	Gina Campbell (and mascots Mr and Mrs Whoppit) sets a new world water speed record at the National Water Sports Centre in Nottingham with an average of 200.88kph. Full Moon
Wednesday *October 10*	BBC TV unveils a brand-new programme called EastEnders which is due to start next January. The building of Albert Square is almost finished on the set at Elstree.
Thursday *October 11*	Dr Kathryn Sullivan becomes the first American woman to walk in space: she spends more than 3hrs outside the shuttle. The brigantine *Zebu* sets sail from the Tower of London at the start of *Operation Raleigh*, a round-the-world expedition for young people.
Friday *October 12*	A new hedgehog service (to be called *St Tiggywinkles*) has been launched at the Wildlife Hospital Trust in Aylesbury, Buckinghamshire. Injured hedgehogs can be sent there by British Rail Red Star!

Saturday *October 13*	The shuttle Challenger, launched on October 5, lands at Kennedy Space Centre in Florida.
Sunday *October 14*	World Conker Championships at Ashton, near Oundle, Northamptonshire 10.30am. The Battle of Hastings is re-enacted with 750 soldiers in full costume at Battle in Sussex 2 pm.
Monday *October 15*	The 1984 Champion Sausage Maker Award goes to David Burns, from Bangor, Co Down.
Tuesday *October 16*	The Princess of Wales is elected President of Barnado's. The Houses of Parliament burned down, 1834.
Wednesday *October 17*	Valentina Tereshkova, who became the 1st spacewoman 21 years ago, is guest of honour at a reception at the Royal Aeronautical Society in London.
Thursday *October 18*	Lord 'Manny' Shinwell becomes the first member of the House of Lords to reach 100!
Friday *October 19*	Two chimps called Billy-Jo and Jennie escape at Colchester Zoo, but are recaptured after 2hrs when they are discovered eating bananas in the kitchen.
Saturday *October 20*	Henry Weston and Robin Cross reach the border between Turkey and Syria on their round-the-world run. They have covered 4827km since they left Tower Bridge on April 1!
Sunday *October 21*	Steve Jones, an RAF corporal from South Wales, sets a new world marathon record in Chicago with a time of 2hr 8min 6secs.
Monday *October 22*	New stamps for Scotland, Wales and N. Ireland go on sale: they include the Scottish Lion, the Welsh Dragon and the Red Hand of Ulster.
Tuesday *October 23*	President Mitterand arrives in Britain for a 4-day State visit. The first pictures of the victims of the famine in Ethiopia are shown on BBC TV.
Wednesday *October 24*	A man is arrested after being chased across the beach in Swansea by two policemen in a 10-tonne digger—top speed 16kph! New Moon
Thursday *October 25*	Ann Houston (9), from John O'Groats, becomes Junior Cook of the Year at the Savoy Hotel in London with a menu of Canisbay Vegetable Broth and Duncawsby Dabs with Green Salad.

Friday October 26	Special food hoppers and nest boxes have been put in Regent's Park, London, for six red squirrels which are released from London Zoo this week! 
Saturday October 27	World Piping Championship at Blair Castle, Blair Atholl, Tayside. The London Championship Cat Show at Pickett's Lock Centre in Edmonton.
Sunday October 28	Summer Time ends at 1am GMT. National Baton-Twirling Championship at Paignton, Devon.
Monday October 29	Twelve British cavers fly to New Britain in Papua New Guinea to explore an underground river – complete with rocket-powered grappling irons.
Tuesday October 30	The Rev Clement Williams celebrates his 105th birthday in Canterbury. A mongrel called Raffles gets his head stuck in a wall in Hartcliffe, Bristol, and has to be freed by firemen!
Wednesday October 31	Heather Couper becomes the first woman president of the British Astronomical Association.

October

 This was the eighth month in the old Roman calendar when the year started in March. The old Dutch name was 'Wyn-maand'—wine month. The old English name was 'Winter-fylleth'—winter full moon.

Pete Marsh's Progress

Peat Bog Man's First Press Conference

Pete Marsh, the only prehistoric body ever found in Britain, is being examined by scientists at the British Museum. He is kept in a specially-built refrigerator at temperatures between 4°C and 7°C and can only be excavated little by little without being damaged. So far, they have discovered that he was garotted before he was buried in the peat bog and that he was about 1.7m tall. He was probably between 20 and 30 years old, had mousey-coloured hair, a red moustache and beard and perfectly manicured nails! It will probably take about 2 years to carry out a full examination of Pete but, after that, he will go on show at the British Museum in London.

Reconstruction of Pete Marsh.

Pete Marsh's Body

November

Thursday *November 1*	Minimum telephone box charges double to 10p today! Warmest November day in London for at least 24 years.
Friday *November 2*	David Attenborough is named Speaker of the Year by the English Speaking Board.
Saturday *November 3*	Torrential rain, floods and landslides in the north of England and Scotland. Rivers burst their banks in Cumbria. A windsurfer at St Ives in Cornwall is knocked off his board by a dolphin.
Sunday *November 4*	A record 330 people leave Hyde Park at 8am at the start of the annual London to Brighton veteran car race. They have to reach Brighton by 4pm!
Monday *November 5*	Victorian Bonfire Night at the Black Country Museum in the Midlands. Typhoon Agnes hits the Philippines—the 18th major storm there this year!
Tuesday *November 6*	State Opening of Parliament 11.30am.
Wednesday *November 7*	St Columba's Abbey on Iona is closed because the 2-tonne bronze bell needs to be repaired. Thanksgiving service in St Paul's Cathedral, London, for the centenary of the NSPCC.
Thursday *November 8*	Esther Rantzen switches on the Christmas lights in Oxford St, London, at 6.30pm. Chay Blyth capsizes south of Cape Horn and is picked up by a Chilean fishing boat. Full Moon
Friday *November 9*	The Department of Transport announces that toad crossing signs are going to be put up next year during the spawning season!
Saturday *November 10*	The *Velsheda*, one of the largest yachts ever built, with a 48.7m mast (almost as tall as Nelson's Column) and sails that would cover a football pitch, goes on view in St Katharine's Docks London.
Sunday *November 11*	Remembrance Sunday: 2 minutes silence to remember the soldiers of World Wars I and II.
Monday *November 12*	The Chancellor of the Exchequer, Nigel Lawson, announces that the Bank of England is to stop issuing £1 notes.
Tuesday *November 13*	The *Sir Walter Raleigh*, flagship of the round-the-world expedition for young people *Operation Raleigh*, sails from Hull.
Wednesday *November 14*	The Christmas lights in Regent St, London, are switched on by Prince Michael of Kent.

November

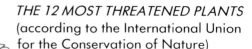

IX This was the ninth month in the old Roman calendar when the year started in March. The old Saxon name was 'Wind-monath'—wind month. The old Dutch name was 'Slaght-maand'—slaughter month. **IX**

THE 12 MOST THREATENED ANIMALS
(according to the International Union for the Conservation of Nature)

* Northern white rhino
  Sumatran rhino
  Orinoco crocodile
  Kouprey wild ox
  Muriqui monkey
* Mediterranean monk seal
* Kagu bird
  Angonoko tortoise
* Hawaian tree snail
  Queen Alexandra birdwing butterfly
  Bumblebee bat
  Pygmy hog

THE 12 MOST THREATENED PLANTS
(according to the International Union for the Conservation of Nature)

African violet (wild)
Bamboo cycad
Drury's slipper orchid
Flor de Mayo shrub
1 Giant rafflesia flower
Kau silversword plant
Neogomesia cactus
2 Philip Island hibiscus
Palenque mahogany
Socotran pomegranate tree
Tarout cypress
3 Yeheb nut bush

November 15th
The new £20 notes are difficult to forge! They have a special metallic security thread which you can see like a row of dashes on the front of the note.

The Post Office issues 5 new Christmas stamps:

DAILY RATTLE 20p
RAF HERCULES TRANSPORT AIRCRAFT BEGIN AIRLIFT OF FOOD TO ETHIOPIA

SQUIGGLE 26p
MINERS RETURN TO WORK

The Gurgle 25p
200,000,000-YEAR-OLD ICHTHYOSAUR DISCOVERED AT ROBIN HOOD'S BAY, NEAR SCARBOROUGH

GRAPEVINE 18p
BRITISH TELECOM'S SALE OF THE CENTURY—THOUSANDS BUY BRITISH TELECOM SHARES

Thursday *November 15*	A new £20 note is available from today!
Friday *November 16*	The International Union for the Conservation of Nature names 12 of the most threatened animals and plants in the world.
Saturday *November 17*	The Trampoline World Cup starts at the National Sports Centre, Crystal Palace, London.
Sunday *November 18*	The Walton Sextuplets celebrate their first birthday in the Wirral, Cheshire.
Monday *November 19*	A Fresian cow called Jasmine is winched up in a net by helicopter after falling 22.8m down a cliff near Ventnor on the Isle of Wight.
Tuesday *November 20*	A flying boat, built in Belfast in 1944, lands in the Medway on her way from Southampton to her winter home in Chatham.
Wednesday *November 21*	A 64-tonne British coaster sinks off Plymouth in Force 9 gales.
Thursday *November 22*	Champion Children Awards at the Savoy Hotel in London. Waves over 6m high crash over sea walls in Kent and Sussex. New Moon
Friday *November 23*	Prince Edward plays 8 different parts in *Captain Curious and His Incredible Quest* in Cambridge.
Saturday *November 24*	A Blue Marlin weighing 649.2kg is caught in Mauritius.
Sunday *November 25*	The world's longest-running play, *The Mousetrap*, celebrates its 32nd birthday! The RAC Rally starts in Chester.
Monday *November 26*	9th Circus World Championship at Wembley. The Great Storm in 1703 killed over 8000 people.
Tuesday *November 27*	Dover Castle is being disguised as the Tower of London for a new film called *Lady Jane Grey*.
Wednesday *November 28*	Paul McCartney receives the Freedom of the City of Liverpool.
Thursday *November 29*	Band Aid's *Do They Know It's Christmas?*, in aid of Ethiopian famine, is released by Phonogram records. It goes straight to No 1 in the charts.
Friday *November 30*	Ned Jago makes his first dive in his home-made mini-submarine— the 2.2m *Xamina*—in the river Axe at Seaton, Devon.

December

Saturday *December 1*	A sponsored walk from Canterbury to London starts to raise money for homeless people at Christmas.
Sunday *December 2*	Daniel Pownall (14 months), from Nutgrove, Liverpool, is crowned Boots Baby of the Year. A 6m whale is washed up on a beach near Weymouth, Dorset.
Monday *December 3*	Zimba, a white rhinoceros, is born at London Zoo.
Tuesday *December 4*	A black crossbred steer called Thunderflash wins the Supreme Cattle Championship at the Royal Smithfield Show at Earl's Court.
Wednesday *December 5*	Brian Cobby wins British Telecom's Golden Voice Competition and will take over from Miss Pat Simmons as the Speaking Clock next spring. It will be the first time that Tim is a man!
Thursday *December 6*	Sebastian Coe and Tessa Sanderson are voted Sportsman and Sportswoman of the Year by the Sports Writers Association.
Friday *December 7*	Vincent Pilkington of Cootehill, Co. Cavan, retains his title of World Champion Turkey Plucker. He plucks a bird in 5min 19secs.
Saturday *December 8*	The 9m skeleton of the first humpback whale to be stranded in Britain (found near Aberthaw, S. Glamorgan) goes on display at the National Museum of Wales in Cardiff. Full Moon
Sunday *December 9*	500 children take part in the Junior Scrabble Championships in London. David Hempleman-Adams leaves for Chile to paddle round Cape Horn in a canoe.
Monday *December 10*	Desmond Tutu, the Anglican bishop of Johannesburg, receives the Nobel Peace Prize in Oslo for his non-violent struggle against apartheid.
Tuesday *December 11*	The tooth of a 120,000,000-year-old iguanodon has been found on the Sussex Downs by Christopher Martin (12), from Lewes.
Wednesday *December 12*	The Advanced Passenger Train sets a rail speed record between Euston and Glasgow: it covers 645.2km in 3hrs 52mins at an average speed of more than 165kph.
Thursday *December 13*	The Christmas tree in Trafalgar Square, London, is lit, 6pm. Tonight is the best night for the Geminid meteor shower!
Friday *December 14*	The Sheriff of Nottingham's golden chain of office is stolen from the Lord Mayor's car.

Saturday *December 15*	The Soviet space craft Vega I is launched on a mission to meet Halley's Comet in March 1986.
Sunday *December 16*	Birdwatchers begin a giant survey of the British coastline to check on winter visitors: about 2,000,000 birds come from as far away as Siberia and Greenland.
Monday *December 17*	Deep snow in the north of England and Scotland. Roads are blocked over the Pennines and motorists are stranded on the A66 between Penrith and Scotch Corner.
Tuesday *December 18*	Top toys for Christmas: Gizmo the Gremlin, Trivial Pursuits, Michael Jackson doll and the A-Team Enforcer van!
Wednesday *December 19*	Ted Hughes (54) is appointed new Poet Laureate: he will get £70 a year and a case of wine. Children of Courage Awards are presented by Princess Anne at Westminster Abbey.
Thursday *December 20*	The Royal Institute of British Architects' Christmas Cake Competition includes entries in the shape of the Royal Pavilion at Brighton, Beachy Head Lighthouse, the Leaning Tower of Pisa and the Penguin Pool at London Zoo.
Friday *December 21*	Shortest day of the year. Prince Henry Charles Albert David (known as Harry) is christened at St George's Chapel, Windsor.
Saturday *December 22*	100 sheep on the Craigdarroch estates in Dumfries and Galloway have been fitted with special synthetic coats from Australia to keep them clean and warm this winter. New Moon
Sunday *December 23*	A baker in Brussels claims the record for the longest Yule Log in the world—164.99m!
Monday *December 24*	About 4,000,000 Christmas trees have been bought in Britain this year: most are Norway spruce although a few fir and pine have been spotted.
Tuesday *December 25*	200 swimmers raise £1700 for charity in a special Christmas Day swim at Hunstanton in Norfolk. Happy Birthday Kenny Everett!
Wednesday *December 26*	Richard and Nick Crane start bicycling up Mount Kilimanjaro in Tanzania to raise money for Intermediate Technology. Black ice closes the A1 in Nottinghamshire for 2hrs.
Thursday *December 27*	A man-made comet, part of a joint British/US/West German project to study how solar winds interact with the earth's magnetic field, explodes 96,540km above the Pacific.

December

This used to be the tenth month in the old Roman calendar when the year started in March.

According to a survey by the British Trust for Ornithology, the numbers of birds in Britain are changing.

Numbers increasing	Numbers decreasing
Mallard	Swallow
Pheasant	Sand martin
Skylark	Whitethroat
Pied wagtail	Corn bunting
Robin	Grey partridge
Nuthatch	
Long-tailed tit	

David Hempleman-Adams becomes the first person to paddle round Cape Horn at the tip of South America. He covers over 320km from Puerto Williams in Chile to Cape Horn Island, which he reaches on December 21.

Richard and Nick Crane ride Saracen ATB mountain bikes up Mount Kilimanjaro (6096m). They have extra low gears and cantilever brakes. Although they have to keep their equipment to a minimum, because of weight, they take a teddy bear mascot with them!

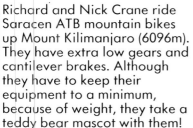

Michael Jackson's album *Thriller* sells a million copies a week in 1984. Seven of the songs on it were issued as singles and they all got into the Top Ten!

The Queen sent 1900 congratulations telegrams to people who reached their 100th birthday in 1984! She sent another 964 to people in the Commonwealth. She also sent 200 messages of congratulations to people who reached their 105th birthdays!

Blabber Mouth 20p
BRITAIN AND CHINA SIGN TREATY RETURNING HONG KONG TO CHINA IN 1997

DAILY QUACK 25p
LEAK FROM CHEMICAL FACTORY AT BHOPAL IN INDIA KILLS AT LEAST 2,000

The Squealer 28p
BRONZE AGE SHIPWRECK DISCOVERED OFF COAST OF TURKEY

DAILY NOD 22p
STRANGE OBJECT SPOTTED IN SKIES BY US INFRA-RED PHOTOGRAPHY: IS IT A BROWN DWARF?

Friday *December 28*	More snow, fog and black ice! The road over Horseshoe Pass, near Llangollen in Wales is closed.
Saturday *December 29*	The first British BMX bike championships are held at the Michael Sobell Centre in London.
Sunday *December 30*	A plaque to George Orwell, who wrote the famous book *1984*, is unveiled at a first-floor flat where he lived in Hampstead.
Monday *December 31*	Goodbye to the ½p coin – it stops being legal tender today! 7,000 people visit the opening day of the 54th Model Engineer Exhibition at Wembley Conference Centre.

CHAMPIONS 1984

Miss Pears	Jenny Currans (3) Hayley Griffiths (7) Jimmy Endicott (6)
Bisto Kids of the Year	
Brownie Guide Tea-making Champion	Lisa Musgrave (9)
Pup of the Year	Champion Filigran the Master of Valetta (a black miniature poodle)
Junior Cook of the Year	Ann Houston (9)
Champion Sausage Maker	David Burns
Bus Driver of the Year	Roy Blaikie
World Ploughing Champion	Desmond Wright
Miss World	Miss Venezuela
Miss UK	Miss Weston-super-Mare
Miss Universe	Miss Sweden
Supreme Champion at Crufts	Hank (a Lhasa Apso)
Mastermind 1984	Margaret Harris
Scrabble Champion	Michael Willis
Pipeman of the Year	Henry Cooper
Pipeman of the Century	Lord Shinwell
King of the Channel	Michael Reid
British Telecom's Golden Voice	Brian Cobby
Museum of the Year	The Quarry Bank Mill, Styal, Cheshire
Jigsaw Puzzle Champion	Barbara Lewis
Sports Writers Association's Sportsman of the Year	Sebastian Coe
Sports Writers Association's Sportswoman of the Year	Tessa Sanderson
Radio 4's Man of the Year	Arthur Scargill
Radio 4's Woman of the Year	Mrs Thatcher
Supreme Cattle Champion	Thunderflash